I0804032

Soccer

LEVEL 0

DECODABLES BY jump!

Teaching Tips

Lilac Level 0

This book focuses on teaching the earliest readers how to read a book by following images and text from left to right.

Before Reading

- Discuss the title. Ask readers what they think the book will be about.

Read the Book

- Encourage readers to describe what they see on each page.
- Ask questions to help readers understand the story and its progression.
    - What happens at the beginning of the book?
    - What happens at the end of the book?
    - How do we know?

After Reading

- Ask readers what part of the book they liked best. Have them find the page or pages that showed this.
- Have readers imagine a different ending for the book. What else could have happened?

This edition is published by arrangement with Booklife Publishing.

North American adaptations © 2024 Jump!
5357 Penn Avenue South
Minneapolis, MN 55419
www.jumplibrary.com

Decodables by Jump! are published by Jump! Library.

Library of Congress Cataloging-in-Publication Data is available at www.loc.gov or upon request from the publisher.

ISBN: 979-8-88996-753-8 (hardcover)
ISBN: 979-8-88996-754-5 (paperback)
ISBN: 979-8-88996-755-2 (ebook)

Photo Credits

Images are courtesy of Shutterstock.com. With thanks to Getty Images, Thinkstock Photo and iStockphoto. Cover – Monkey Business Images, p4–5 – PeopleImages.com - Yuri A, swissdrone, p6–7 – Monkey Business Images, p8–9 – Monkey Business Images, p10–11 – Monkey Business Images, hxdbzxy, p12 – Monkey Business Images.

About Reading

When we read a book, we go from left to right, like this:

Some books just have pictures, like this:

Some books have words and pictures, like this:

Close the book and flip it over to read Ballet!

Ballet

LEVEL 0

DECODABLES BY jump!

Teaching Tips

Lilac Level 0

This book focuses on teaching the earliest readers how to read a book by following images and text from left to right.

Before Reading

- Discuss the title. Ask readers what they think the book will be about.

Read the Book

- Encourage readers to describe what they see on each page.
- Ask questions to help readers understand the story and its progression.
    - What happens at the beginning of the book?
    - What happens at the end of the book?
    - How do we know?

After Reading

- Ask readers what part of the book they liked best. Have them find the page or pages that showed this.
- Have readers imagine a different ending for the book. What else could have happened?

North American adaptations © 2024 Jump!
5357 Penn Avenue South
Minneapolis, MN 55419
www.jumplibrary.com

Library of Congress Cataloging-in-Publication Data is available at www.loc.gov or upon request from the publisher.

ISBN: 979-8-88996-753-8 (hardcover)
ISBN: 979-8-88996-754-5 (paperback)
ISBN: 979-8-88996-755-2 (ebook)

Photo Credits

Images are courtesy of Shutterstock.com. With thanks to Getty Images, Thinkstock Photo and iStockphoto. Cover – ucchie79. p4–5 – Lana K, Maryna Kulchytska, p6–7 – Sean Nel, ucchie79, p8–9 – Maria Moroz, Maryna Kulchytska, p10–11 –JoHo, Photobac, p12 – BearFotos.

About Reading

When we read a book, we go from left to right, like this:

Some books just have pictures, like this:

Some books have words and pictures, like this:

Close the book and flip it over to read Soccer!